MASTEREARTH of Maitreya Buddha proposes to supplant the capital system

I0698216

Replace the monetary unit with qualified time units and assign minimum life annuities

Cover image: pxhere.com

Published by: Roberto Guillermo Gomes

Contact: yogi.mettatron@gmail.com

Published Worldwide

"Robotics annuls the system of capital and work, from there you can choose between redistributing wealth equally among all inhabitants or hyper-concentrating it in a few hands and leaving the masses in misery, in uncertainty and to their own fate." Maitreya Buddha's Dhammapada. 2153

INDEX

INTRODUCTION

THE CAPITAL SYSTEM HAS REACHED A LIMIT POINT OF IRREVERSIBILITY IN RELATION TO THE ENVIRONMENT, FROM WHICH INTERNAL DISECONOMIES OF SCALE ARE PRODUCED ON PRODUCTION SYSTEMS BASED ON EXTERNAL ECOLOGICAL CAUSES. THAT IS TO SAY, PRODUCTION GOODS TEND TO RAISE THEIR COSTS. THIS IS ALREADY NOTICED IN THE RISING PRICES OF FOOD, IN THE VALUES OF REAL PROPERTY AND OTHER VITAL INPUTS. THE COST IS STOPPING BEING EFFECTIVE AND THIS IS PAID BY THE MOST IMPOVERISHED POPULATION.

How is the process?: Here we give an example:

A farmer cuts down a patch of rain forest, plants crops, and reaps a bountiful harvest. He is immediately imitated by the other men in his village, until they wipe out a large area of that same rain forest. As a consequence, the rainfall regime is modified, the drought arrives, the land becomes arid and dry. Then the crops no longer yield.

This is exactly what Humanity is now doing to all of nature on our planet Earth, overexploiting natural resources, under the pressure of overpopulation demand. Ending in the short time of one to two generations with the ecological net worth of an entire planet. This has direct and indirect effects on the behavior of regional, national and international economies, causing disruptions. Which will intensify in the same proportion as renewable and non-renewable resources begin to become severely scarce.

ANTIDOTES

The first antidote to the crisis is the control and progressive reduction of overpopulation. Within a limited world, population with unlimited tendency cannot be sustained. The planet has the carrying capacity to give life support to about 5,000 million human beings. The ideal would be a billion. That is the goal. Along the way, the restriction on new births should be imposed. For example, only legally allow couples to have only one child and penalize transgressions. There is no other solution. The subject is annoying, but there is no other alternative than to apply it or we will destroy our ecosystem under penalty of self-extinction.

The second antidote consists in passing from the accumulation of egotistical capital to the system of shared solidarity capital. Here too there is no room for another alternative. It is the hyper-concentrated capital system that is destroying the Earth's reserves, feeding the infernal machinery of hyper-consumption. As long as we allow it to continue to operate, it will continue to undermine our life support. This is necessary to understand. Carry out educational campaigns so that the entire population can understand it. We must change the system or we will not survive.

But first we must know how to see that we owe to the current capital system the efficiency that makes the productive machinery of the world work. What makes possible that on our table and in our home are the products of the most distant regions and nations, that sowing and harvesting are carried out in a timely manner, the transport of merchandise, both by land, sea and air, that there is an effective marketing system… All this is positive. But the excessive desire for profit is gradually killing us, causing the 6th Mass Extinction of all species. We must know how to stop ourselves and get out of the system.

Get out of the system? It is easy to say, putting it into practice is difficult and for which the combined effort of all world actors is required, the union of all power factors, once the need for change has been fully understood, its nature , its meaning and direction.

MONEY IS AN ABSTRACTION OF HUMAN ENERGY

Money is an abstract convention that represents human work or energy. By means of surplus value, interest can be accumulated on capital and in this way money can be multiplied. Within a cybernetic society, money can be directly replaced by real value, that is, qualified time. This will eliminate the poor and the millionaires at the same time, universalizing a middle class with a high standard of quality of life.

Electronic media will allow devices such as the cell phone, which can be used in bracelets or in augmented reality glasses, to serve as a support for instant transactions (this already exists). For example, a bracelet can be used that interacts with the user's DNA only. The device will automatically load credits for qualified time corresponding to each month. The person will be able to make their purchases and simply pass the chip inserted in the bracelet to the store's digital cash register and thus complete the purchase.

The same can be done through the cell phone and the PC, with specific digital software.

The most creative subjects within society will be the ones who will be able to accumulate the greatest amount of credit and enjoy greater access to the different services. Knowledge will be rewarded and there will be no more need to do business. Since there is no more money, it will no longer be the main goal to accumulate it. The new pattern of objectives will be scientific and artistic merits.

About how the system will work, those who accumulate the greatest amount of credits, by being more proactive, will be able to access the community assets. For example, to the Hubble telescope, in the event that the citizen is a scientist, and to have this support to carry out field research.

Speculation, capital gains and banks will be prohibited. Everyone will enjoy a guaranteed minimum income for life, since the production system, in all repetitive areas, will have been transferred to robots and AIs. In this way, everyone will have their basic needs guaranteed, in accordance with universal rights.

In turn, in the restructuring of world society, every citizen at birth should enjoy the following guaranteed free rights:

1. Full access to health.

2. Full access to a healthy diet.

3. Total free and open access to education.

4. Full access to decent housing.

5. Full access to decent work.

6. Full access to digitized government.

7. Full access to settle in the place of the world of your free choice.

The money will not exist, as compensation for the basic universal rights, each individual is obliged to pay an hourly load to provide specific community services, within the new emerging system. Since repetitive and physical tasks are performed by robots, humans are engaged in intellectual and creative actions. This social model will be common at the end of this 21st century.

This will be complemented with 100% security, through advanced digital technology that allows the advances of Human-X Technologies applications in the field of high personal, urban and interurban security, of maximum scope and level.

Crime is reduced to a minimum percentage, through the interactive logic of the hyper-concentrated convergence of the new digital media.

This external aspect, in turn, is reinforced by the Ahimsa Program, which allows a satellite network bathing the entire planetary surface, with constant flows of frequencies adjusted to brain waves to produce coherent alpha mental wave operation and therefore, with less content of aggression and violence, individual and collective.

It should also be understood that the concept of free universal rights, endorsed by its Single Planetary Magna Carta, are counterbalanced by strict obligations within the logic of the new socioeconomic, political, scientific and military system.

Every individual has an obligation to be productively active and useful to the system. The customizable individual benefit levels for him are based on the greater logic of service to the collective community of which he is a part.

And this service is impartially registered and evaluated by the processing of constant exchanges of neurodigital flows. The system only closes, likewise, if it is under the structural format of Direct Digital Democracy, full citizen freedom, full citizen power.

I call this form of self-government Solidaricracy; that is, the superior logic of the system responds to Compassion, as a functionality that allows the different levels of growth of the high complexity of the socioeconomic machinery.

The psychological pattern, the core programming in the deep collective subconscious, at the subliminal and surface levels, is Compassion, replacing doctrines and other limited thought forms. This allows Sacred Life Defense to be the priority of the entire system.

And so, the primordial rights of individuals and all planetary citizens are defended by the integrality of the collective system of which they are a part.

Within the organization every citizen has the right to a plate of basic nutritious food on a daily basis, no citizen should die from lack of food. This is an act of maximum crime.

Those responsible are immediately arrested and tried publicly and openly. The death penalty does not exist, because in an advanced culture it is understood that no one has the right to take life.

Life is Sacred and must be respected, otherwise coherence with the force of superior unity is lost, through the logic of Compassion. God gives us life, only God takes it from us. Once technology allows it, the execution of criminals will consist of the erasure of their sick psychological self from its cerebral support and the implantation of another healthy and positive one.

And how will the money be? First let's start from what money is, in essence. It is an abstraction about units of energy in the real world. Such units are equivalent to seconds, minutes and hours of work of an average human being. This understanding allows us to see money as a way of accelerating exchanges on given flows of exchanges of energy flows, which represent materialized modifications on the real world, objects and concrete functions. Money = time.

This being the reality of the economic system, the logical evolution is to get rid of money as a standard of exchange and concentrate on units of time.

The reason for this is that money, as it is now on the world, represents an already inefficient model, with a high loss of energy charge in the exchange processes, equivalent to charge transmission. These voltage losses cause job losses and internal contradictions in the system, that is, voltage jumps and transformer bursts, equivalent to speculation, financial usury, the cost of money itself and cyclical economic crises. All this can be overcome by changing the model directly. (And by proceeding with the exchange, the internal and external debts of the States may be liquefied...).

It cannot be overcome within the money model, because they are contradictions inherent in the model. What can we rationally and logically do to evolve? Substitute money for units of superiorly qualified time, of thinking human productivity.

In other words, in accordance with the 7 Basic Human Rights, every citizen is guaranteed the availability of units of time, within the collective logic of the system that they integrate, and thus their basic needs for life and development are guaranteed.

Now, qualified time as a unit of exchange allows, through high-integration digital support, that the individual production of increasing qualification is cumulative.

This does not allow the proprietary accumulation of the previous monetary system, but rather greater access to sufficient and necessary technological means, which in turn allow greater development in individual levels of qualification.

For example, if a citizen has a highly developed mind, he may have access, for example, to the commands of the Hubble telescope, to complete explorations and research projects, as we have already explained. This is by way of example as it responds to a Knowledge Society model.

The accumulation of qualified time is also used for transactions or exchanges of differentiated selective products. If the average citizen makes a greater effort, he obtains greater benefits.

This is adjusted with your electronic service sheet. The system can give rise to new forms of crime, this is foreseen in the development of custom hardware and software.

And even so, if possible criminals appear when they are located, they are expelled to lawless cities, thus eliminating penitential centers. Where they are forced to live in conditions of inferior technology, in underworlds.

This substitution of money for qualified time represents an enormous leap for present Humanity, even greater than the first step taken on the Moon. Because this new logic of exchange and transaction flows will release enormous reserves of psychological energy, human psychic force and neutralized or underutilized potentialities in urban parks and centers of specialized industrial production.

We should all reflect that a system where corporations like Microsoft can disappear from one day to the next is not rational.

The capital system reached its maximum level of development, now it is time to perfect it and replace it with a logic of a higher order, more rational, more supportive, more ecological.

If everyone who works at Microsoft is freed from the pressure of vital survival, they can focus on higher goals, as NASA does.

Even NASA, if it counts on the constant readjustment of its budgets, depending on the greater strategies and impacts contemplated, it will be able to better concentrate on achieving its objectives.

In other words, the logic of money, the hyper-concentration of capital resources allowed us, from the transfer of American gold to the treasures of Spain and then Holland, France and England, the process of industrialization. But the power of money was exhausted. And now it is dangerous to continue organizing the human race, its societies, under this archaic pattern. We have digital technology, we must know how to apply it for superior purposes and objectives.

President Obama convened the world's heads of state, as well as business leaders and non-governmental organizations for an open debate in December 2009, to increase the logic of global employment. Pointing out that the full reactivation of the intrinsic dynamics of the North American economy is necessarily complemented by the world economy that national economies build through their exchange flows in international trade.

The 1x1 Program is essential to establish a new labor market logic. The program allows the fusion between constant training channels and objective production just in time. It is a model that will grow and absorb the entire flow of market transformations shortly, based on the expansive wave of digitization of human production tasks.

It's just stopping to think for a moment and being able to see clearly that we are going from the model of Pablo Flintstone, working in the quarry, to the Super Sonic Family, with Super interacting with an intelligent industrial computer.

If we do not apply now, with total decision, the model of the 1x1 Program, we will pay very heavily for the consequences (with massive international structural unemployment), which will be caused by the cybernetic wave led by the United States.

In the 1x1 Program in co-participation teleworking on capital gains, people registered in the system work one hour a day and receive in return a fixed percentage share of the profits of the companies that hire them.

Our educational and work models are separate and are like Pedro Flintstone, prehistoric, that is, pre-digital, because we use notebooks in schools, it does not mean that the system that we integrate is intelligently digital.

This new model can be implemented as a pilot test in Miami, Belo Horizonte and in some city in Jordan.

The reason for these 3 cities responds to the logic of the average moral evolution of their towns; given that greater moral intelligence is a sine qua non condition for a greater integral evolution of average intelligences and access to high technologies.

This pattern can be quickly replicated in Tokyo, Beijing, Singapore, Frankfurt, and London, then spread across the planet.

It must be understood that the qualitative changes that Humanity urgently needs now, cannot be obtained under models that can be immediately massified.

It must first be experienced in a few cities and then transferred to the planetary collective society. Under this logic, the hyper-concentration of new models and technological parameters is simple and effective.

We cannot create the future supertechnological society in all human cities at the same time, but we can in a few experimental ones, whose number of inhabitants, their infrastructure of resources and their digital culture allow and admit it.

THE SCOURGE OF LOW IQ

The greatest scourge of present Humanity, and of which almost nobody talks, is the low average IQ of the population. This condition of the collective intelligence of the masses is the reason for their irrational reactions, for domestic and criminal violence, for war and for all kinds of aggression. Let's see the situation:

Percentage of the population with IQ

IQ	%	Level
130	2.1	Very gifted
121-130	6.4	Gifted
111-120	15.7	Intelligence above average

90-110	51.6	Average intelligence
80-89	15.7	Intelligence below average
70-79	6.4	Mental retardation

- Source: Resing en Blok (2002)

Only 0.5% of the population has a mental coefficient above 140 points. While those who reach 180 points are considered geniuses.

So it is a priority to move from the consumer society to the Knowledge Society. Where 80% of the audiovisual media are dedicated to training and knowledge and only 20% of the content to entertainment.

Furthermore, medical science, genetics, and molecular biology are constantly advancing. Neuronal regeneration will be possible in the future. Artificially increasing the number of synapses and neurochips will allow direct link between neurons and AI, increasing personal IQ to off-scale limits. We are on the verge of an evolutionary leap, so great that it will leave Homo Sapiens behind and we will become a new species. But if we err along the way and fall into dead ends, we can self-extinguish...

Space exploration is beginning to design highly functional and technological futuristic cities. These models can be applied on Planet Earth for the reconversion of urban parks and thus build the civilization of the XXII century.

IMAGINE A BETTER WORLD

With the Master Plan to Save the Planet we project a world without hunger, without poverty, without pandemics, without borders, with 2 languages, one universal, with a single Army and therefore without wars, without currency and without capital, with an Eco Government Planetarium under the Global Direct Digital Democracy system, where the citizens of the world vote on all laws and appoint and dismiss the authorities of the other central powers, advised by a Council of Sciences made up of the best scientists from all continents, with the work in charge of cybernetics and AI, redistributing the benefits through a life annuity to the entire employed population through creative leisure and social, artistic and scientific service.

Adults, children and the elderly, meditating and expanding their minds to Cosmic Quantum Intelligence. With the planet greened through the recovery of forests and oceans, along with the protection of biodiversity.

Finally, man living in peace and brotherhood with each other and in harmony between science, technology and Nature... We just have to wake up, unite and together make it a reality.

HOW TO MAKE IT A REALITY?

We can only achieve this by joining forces and initiatives for world peace and progress. And do it from inside the capital system, not against it, not from outside. It is the only way to gradually transform the model and convert it into a system of Solidarity Capital of Equal Distribution.

What do we mean by this definition? We refer to the minimum life annuity that will be necessary to implement on the human population when the production and work systems are transferred to robots and AIs. Something that will happen overnight.

Suddenly, the assembly lines of the humanoid robots that will replace us will begin to function and will be assembled en masse. Very quickly they will evolve and become smarter, more skilled, more productive and will displace human labor.

The new neurochips, better and more powerful memories will make a difference. In turn, errorless quantum computing will support more powerful AIs.

Within this cyber world that the immediate future holds for us, Telecommuting is our last work refuge and towards it we must emigrate en masse as quickly as possible in an efficient and organized manner.

From the Universal Religion, it is proposed as an alternative solution to make donations and capital contributions to activate

Teleworking multi-portals and transfer 50% of the net profits to UNICFEF and other NGOs.

For the system to be understood, this is different from making donations to charities or to the poor, who will continue to need help because their structural living conditions are not altered.

With the donations and capital contributions, multi-portals are activated that first create hundreds and then thousands, hundreds of thousands of Telecommuting positions within the Internet connected to E-Commerce and E-Business. This gives our daily bread to the different active members of each portal.

And with 50% of the profits, aid and direct financial aid is provided to NGOs such as UNICEF, CARITAS, INTERNATIONAL RED CROSS, DOCTORS WITHOUT BORDERS and the initiative LET'S PLANT 30 BILLION TREES PER YEAR.

In this way, a proactive Solidarity Capital system is created. Philanthropists and humanitarian foundations are no longer needed, the system is in charge of providing the necessary resources.

And in addition, all the information related to income, movements of resources, investments and donations, is published in full online in public form. That is our commitment.

The first step consists of a donation or capital contribution equivalent to 1 million dollars free of taxes. It will be used in the registration of Universal Religion as such, which will make it possible to function with tax exemption and in the creation of the Global Solidarity Foundation for the administration of the Humanitarian Marketing Program project.

For capital contributions, the possible partners of the system receive benefits equivalent to 50% of the net profits, discounting the necessary projected reinvestments for each particular case.

The First Turn of Modern Sacred Dharma is not religious on the surface. It is applied to the system of capital and work, on which our daily bread depends. It perfects it, massifies it and solidifies it, allowing a higher state of mind and spirit to be reached.

Every member of the Telework teams of this community is invited to be part of the 8 pillars of the Universal Religion and to practice Contemplative Neuroscience on a daily basis. Thus, the transformation is complete, encompassing the triple reality of body, mind and soul.

CALL OF CONSCIENCE

If you are a billionaire, I call on you, I need your help and collaboration to positively change the world. I give you the opportunity to participate in a revolutionary transformation of the planetary life system that we all inhabit.

From the Universal Religion, as Buddha Maitreya, I propose the Egalitarian Solidarity Capital. This will translate into a minimum life annuity for the benefit of all citizens of the world.

No! It's not communism, it's Proactive Solidarity. We all need to understand that the capital system, on which we all depend to eat, dress, work, get ahead and live, has reached its ultimate breaking point. The diseconomies implied in said system are destroying our world, our ecological sustainability through superfluous hyper-consumption. And also generating conditions of social intensification of personal violence and between nations.

The new replacement system consists of exchanging the money standard for qualified time. Each world citizen, in exchange for their community service provided during their active week, receives qualifying time credits. Which are electronically loaded into a bracelet in digital form, to be worn on the wrist, which is inviolable, because it operates using the user's DNA as a key.

About what to do with the rich, millionaires and billionaires... All of them will be able to continue enjoying their assets and fortunes as long as they live, but they will not be able to leave them as an inheritance. When they die, their assets will go to the Solidarity Capital system.

As a yogi I cannot eat more than my stomach space allows. I can't wear more than one pair of shoes at a time. Like pants and a shirt. I cannot inhabit more than one house at the same time. I only need to be able to eat, dress, study and meditate, nothing more... So, if you are a billionaire, why do you want so many millions, if you cannot buy the Kingdom of Heaven when you die?

Instead of being remembered as a successful person, wouldn't it be better to be remembered as a caring and caring person? So think about it, help me to give the First Turn in the Modern Wheel of the Sacred Dharma for the benefit of the entire Humanity.

BIBLIOGRAPHIC REFERENCES

Benians, E. A. (1925). "II. Adam Smith's Project of an Empire". Cambridge Historical Journal. 1 (3): 249–283. doi:10.1017/S1474691300001062.

Bonar, James, ed. (1894). A Catalogue of the Library of Adam Smith. London: Macmillan. OCLC 2320634 – via Internet Archive.

Buchan, James (2006). The Authentic Adam Smith: His Life and Ideas. W.W. Norton & Company. ISBN 0-393-06121-3.

Buchholz, Todd (1999). New Ideas from Dead Economists: An Introduction to Modern Economic Thought. Penguin Books. ISBN 0-14-028313-7.

Bussing-Burks, Marie (2003). Influential Economists. Minneapolis: The Oliver Press. ISBN 1-881508-72-2.

Campbell, R.H.; Skinner, Andrew S. (1985). Adam Smith. Routledge. ISBN 0-7099-3473-4.

Coase, R.H. (October 1976). "Adam Smith's View of Man". The Journal of Law and Economics. 19 (3): 529–46. doi:10.1086/466886. S2CID 145363933.

Helbroner, Robert L. The Essential Adam Smith. ISBN 0-393-95530-3

Nicholson, J. Shield (1909). A project of empire;a critical study of the economics of imperialism, with special reference to the ideas of Adam Smith. hdl:2027/uc2.ark:/13960/t4th8nc9p.

Otteson, James R. (2002). Adam Smith's Marketplace of Life. Cambridge: Cambridge University Press. ISBN 0-521-01656-8

Palen, Marc-William (2014). "Adam Smith as Advocate of Empire, c. 1870–1932" (PDF). The Historical Journal. 57: 179–198. doi:10.1017/S0018246X13000101. S2CID 159524069. Archived from the original (PDF) on 18 February 2020.

Rae, John (1895). Life of Adam Smith. London & New York: Macmillan. ISBN 0-7222-2658-6. Retrieved 14 May 2018 – via Internet Archive.

Ross, Ian Simpson (1995). The Life of Adam Smith. Oxford University Press. ISBN 0-19-828821-2.

Ross, Ian Simpson (2010). The Life of Adam Smith (2 ed.). Oxford University Press.

Skousen, Mark (2001). The Making of Modern Economics: The Lives and Ideas of Great Thinkers. M.E. Sharpe. ISBN 0-7656-0480-9.

Smith, Adam (1977) [1776]. An Inquiry into the Nature and Causes of the Wealth of Nations. University of Chicago Press. ISBN 0-226-76374-9.

Smith, Adam (1982) [1759]. D.D. Raphael and A.L. Macfie (ed.). The Theory of Moral Sentiments. Liberty Fund. ISBN 0-86597-012-2.

Smith, Adam (2002) [1759]. Knud Haakonssen (ed.). The Theory of Moral Sentiments. Cambridge University Press. ISBN 0-521-59847-8.

- # NEUROYOGA: GLOBAL GOALS

1. Planetary Government
2. Global Direct Digital Democracy
3. Impersonate money for qualified time
4. Green Fund of 3% of annual world GDP
5. Abolish poverty
6. Zero hunger
7. Minimum annuity against cybernetics
8. Climate action
9. Recovery of forests and oceans
10. Protect ecosystems
11. Save the Arctic and Amazon
12. Clean water and sanitation
13. Sustainable cities and communities
14. Sustainable Industry, Innovation and Infrastructure
15. Responsible consumption and production
16. Intensive development of renewable energies
17. Fusion reactors
18. Safe AI development
19. Health and wellness
20. Quality education
21. Guaranteed work and economic growth
22. Reduction of inequalities
23. Gender equality

24.   Peace, justice and strong institutions

25.   Union for biosustainability

*** Inspired by the UN Millennium Goals**

Roberto Guillermo Gomes

Máster Maitreya Buddha

Architect / Journalist / Auctioneer and Public Broker / Graphic Designer / Web Designer / Fisherman Sailor / Ecologist / Writer / Master's Degree in Astronomy and Astrophysics / Master's Degree in Cognitive Neuroscience / Master's Degree in Psychology / Master's Degree in Yoga / Master's Degree in Acupuncture, Osteopathy, Natural Therapies, Therapeutic Yoga / Master in Mindfulness and Relaxation in the Educational Field / Professor in Mindfulness / Professional Mindfulness Technician / University Yoga Monitor / Infant Yoga Monitor / Postgraduate in Neuro-linguistic Programming NLP / Specialist in Data Analysis and Statistical Techniques in Astrophysics / Specialist in Stellar Atmospheres / Specialist in Galactic and Extragalactic Physics / Professional Technician in Ayurvedic Abhyanga and Bioenergetic Massage / Ayurvedic teacher / Specialist in Cranial Osteopathy / Acupuncture Technician / Specialist in Relaxation and Breathing Techniques / Expert in Cognitive Neuroscience / Technician in Child Care Psychology / Technician in Child Care Psychology / Technician in Child Care Psychology Tem prana / Technician in Psycho-educational Intervention in Behavior Alterations in Children 0-13 years old / Technician in Natural Therapies / Postgraduate Therapeutic Yoga Monitor / Expert in Fundamental Ethical, Philosophical and Mystical Principles of Yoga / Expert in Asana and Pranayama , Sequences and Progressions (Vinyasa and Karana) / Expert in Relaxation and Meditation in Yoga / Expert in Diagnostic Analysis and Evaluation in Instruction in Yoga / Specialist Technician in Programming and Resource Management in Instructional Activities in Yoga / Specialist in Design and Direction of Sessions and Activities of Yoga / Sports Coaching / Expert in Mindfulness in the Classroom / Technician in Neuropsychology of Education / MBSR (Mindfulness Based Stress Reduction) (41 university and tertiary degrees).

Creator of NeuroYoga. Developer of the FlashBrain Program for intellectual growth, the Sophia system and the Synaptic Meditation technique. Promoter and leader of the initiative for 2% of world GDP, annually, to provide a definitive solution to the triple scourge of hunger, overpopulation and global warming.

He was born in Argentina, in 1956. He had his first spiritual trance at 16 years of age. At 17, the Virgin appeared to him and asked him **"Why don't you believe in Me?"** Shortly after, the Cosmic Mother, was awakening different states of high samadhis and had spiritual experiences very similar to those of Paramahansa Ramakrishna. At age 19, he became a disciple of Yogananda and in meditation, he rediscovered the ancient Kriya technique. He studied TM with the Maharishi and Zazen with Master Bustamante.

Yogi affirms that **"my experiences with God are the derivative of a contact with the essence of my own spiritual Being, since the soul and God share the same substratum of existence. They are a transcendent step in the knowledge of oneself. The phenomenon is it finds itself within the mental field and is its reflection".**

Subsequently, he completed his training as a graphic designer, journalist, auctioneer and public runner, fisherman sailor, architect, web designer, writer, master in yoga and creator of NeuroYoga.

On 02/02/04, after a prolonged period of meditation with the Vipassana technique, he reached mental cessation.

He designed the Sophia system, from Cerebral Synergy, by means of which it is possible to redesign the brain by stimulating neuroplasticity and increasing the IQ. He synthesized the Synaptic Meditation technique, by which accumulated stress is discharged, diseases are prevented and memory, attention and intelligence are increased, allowing the Superbrain to function.

Its objective is to westernize the millenary spiritual knowledge of the East without losing the essence of its nucleus, expanding and renewing the investigation. Simplify meditation, making it available to everyone and laying the foundations for its introduction to the curriculum in world education systems.

The other focus is to unite actions to stop Global Warming-

Flooding, while there is still time to apply preventive and corrective measures to the situation presented by greenhouse gases. At the same time expanding compassion to address the scourge of hunger, which punishes more than a billion, and educating to stop overpopulation.

"My mission: to serve humanity"

Yogi Mettàtron is Western and Christian. He successfully achieved two careers in his life: one as a journalist, becoming editor-in-chief of a newspaper, and the other as a practicing yogi. His work was always focused on serving others. For him, serving is "the highest expression of Love."

Through the teachings of Vedanta he gradually discovered what the true goal of life was. On 02/02/04, after a prolonged period of meditation with the Vipassana technique, he reached mental cessation, when consciousness merges with the Absolute. He wanted to help people both physically, mentally, and spiritually. This is how he created the NeuroYoga system, a yoga of synthesis that creates the basis for modern yoga practice in the West.

The greatest treasure is knowledge

Writing became Yogi Mettàtron's new mission. So he was able to bring people more lasting help. His goal is to spread spiritual knowledge as much as possible. For him knowledge is the greatest of all gifts. The words we hear are soon forgotten; only the written word endures.

He has written the series «Advaita Meditation», where the union between God and the Soul is enunciated, where to know one's own Being is to realize the Absolute in Oneself. He is currently working on the "Meditation Tutorials" collection consisting of 50 books, where the science of contemplation is explained in detail. In the project are the series "Mindfulness Action", "Yoga Fitness", "Neuroyoga Data", "Budismo Data" and "A walk through the Cosmos". As well as several novels.

During his almost 25 years of journalism, he wrote some 19,360 articles, notes, interviews and chronicles; Due to that training he has the capacity to write a book per month.

He published 90 books in 3 years, 29 in 2019, 10 in 2020 and 51 in 2021, from March 2019 to March 2022. An average of 30 books per year. He also wrote "Option Zero" and then "Gaia Maligna", in just one day. While for the "First turn in the wheel of the modern Holy Dharma" he took 3 hours.

Other writers have taken more than 30 years to write more than 90 books. Gomes took just over 10% of that time.

Holistic Yoga

Teaches Yoga from a holistic point of view: NeuroYoga teaches us to strengthen and harmonize the body, mind and soul, so that we can achieve the goal: a healthy body, a balanced mind and inner peace. NeuroYoga helps remove inner obstacles and gives us strength to stay level-headed, calm, and connected when faced with the daily challenges of modern life.

yogi.mettatron@gmail.com